Writing

Library of Congress Number: 80-15334

2 3 4 5 6 7 8 9 0 88 87 86 85 84

Printed in the United States of America.

Library of Congress Cataloging in Publication Data

Allington, Richard L
 Writing.

 (Beginning to learn about)
 SUMMARY: Situations taken from daily life
demonstrate the usefulness and pleasure of writing.
 1. Writing — Juvenile literature. 2. Communication
— Juvenile literature. [1. Writing. 2. Communication]
I. Krull, Kathleen, joint author. II. Miyake, Yoshi.
III. Title. IV. Series.
P211.A62   808'.042   80-15334
ISBN 0-8172-1321-X

Richard L. Allington is Associate Professor, Department of Reading,
State University of New York at Albany.
Kathleen Krull is the author of nineteen books for children.

BEGINNING TO LEARN ABOUT

WRITING

BY RICHARD L. ALLINGTON, PH.D., · AND KATHLEEN KRULL

ILLUSTRATED BY YOSHI MIYAKE

Raintree Childrens Books · Milwaukee · Toronto · Melbourne · London

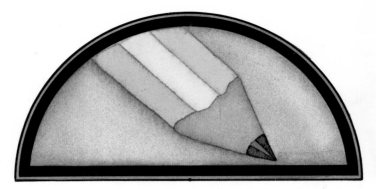

Have you ever wondered why we write?
This story will show you some of the
reasons. Can you think of others?

We use the alphabet for writing.
Can you say the letters? Can you
trace them with your finger?

A a B b C c D d

E e F f G g H h

I i J j K k L l

M m N n O o

P p Q q R r S s

T t U u V v

W w X x Y y Z z

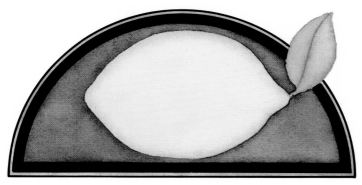

In the summer, I sell lemonade. I want people to see my lemonade stand. What should I do?

Scream?

Have my dog do tricks?

Write a sign?

7

Then I go on a trip with my family.
I want to keep a record of my trip.
What can I do?

Write a diary?

Aug. 3

Today we saw
a castle.
It looked very
ol

Read a book?

Build a model?

Soon it is time for school to start. On the first day, I see that my sister has a jacket just like mine. What should I do to make sure our jackets don't get mixed up?

Wear my jacket inside out?

Write our names on them?

Take my sister's jacket away from her?

At school, I make up a ghost story.
By the time I get to the middle,
I can't remember the beginning
anymore. What should I do?

Feel scared?

Decide to read a book instead?

The ghost was
big and mean.
The ghost lived
in an old
haunted house

Write the story down?

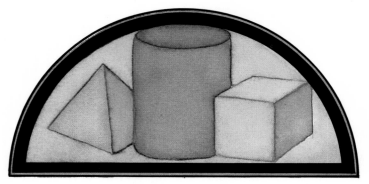

In math class, I always forget what the shapes are called. What can I do to help me remember?

Ask my friends?

Write labels?

Count to ten?

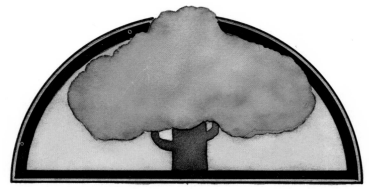

Sometimes we have a test in school.
I know the answers to the questions.
What should I do?

Write the answers?

Shout the answers?

Draw the answers?

We visit the library. The librarian tells us to be quiet. But I see a spider crawling toward my friend. What should I do?

Look for a book about spiders?

Write a note?

Scream?

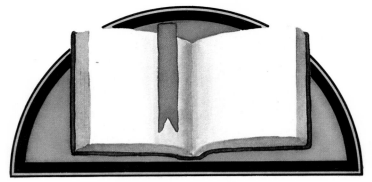

We read a good book in reading class.
I wish the author of the book knew
how much I like it. What can I do?

Tear out some pages and
put them on my wall?

Write a letter to the author?

Read the book again and again?

On the way home from school, I
have to buy five things at the store.
What should I do to make sure
I don't forget anything?

Buy everything I see?

Keep saying the things over and over?

Write a list?

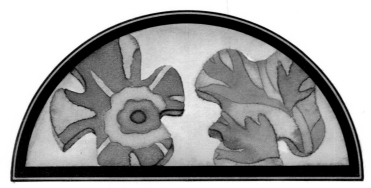

After school, I work on a jigsaw puzzle. One of the pieces is missing. What should I do?

Get mad and kick the puzzle?

Write a letter to the company
that made the puzzle?

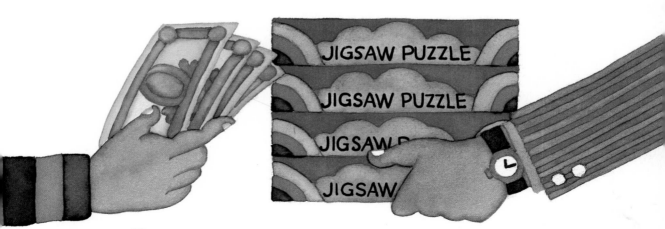

Buy more puzzles to see if the
missing piece is in them?

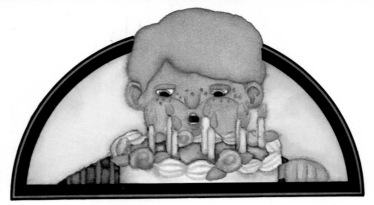

I remember that my best friend's birthday is coming up. He lives far away now. What can I do?

Write a birthday card?

Play "Happy Birthday" on the piano?

Tell him happy birthday
the next time I see him?

I want to tell my friend how to make
our favorite cookies. What can I do?

Take a picture of the cookies?

Send him a cookie in the mail?

Write a recipe for him?

Then I go to bed. I dream that I am alone on an island. How should I get help?

Go swimming?

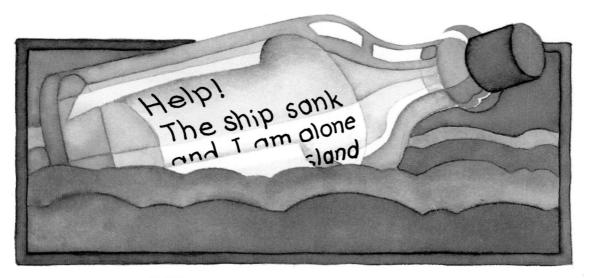

Write a note and put
it in a bottle?

Cry a lot?

Make your own writing book.
Look at a newspaper or magazine.
Cut out pictures of things you like.
Try to find pictures of things whose
words begin with each letter of the alphabet.
Tape or paste the pictures onto pieces of paper.
Underneath each picture, write down the word
that matches the picture. Fasten the papers
together in order of the alphabet.
You may ask an adult to help you.

Write down your name, your phone number, and
your address.
Can you think of five reasons why you would need to
write these?
You may ask an adult to help you.